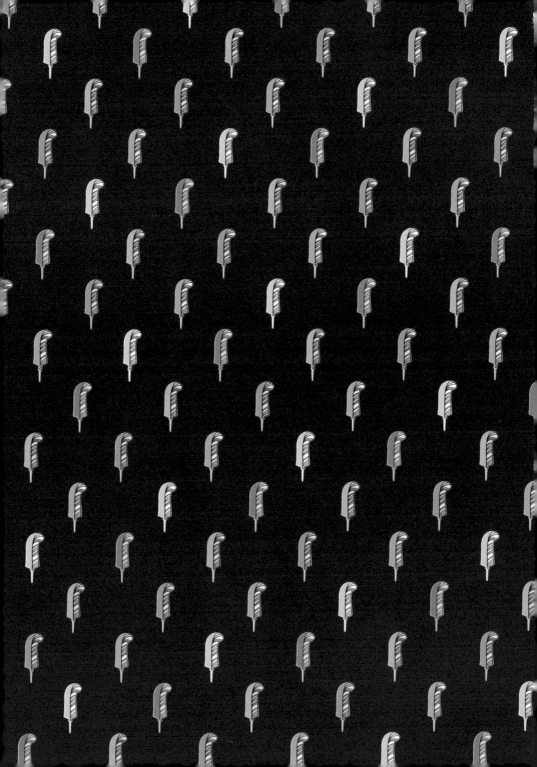

EVERYDAY
AMENTI

A GUIDED JOURNAL FOR
CULTIVATING A FEATHER-LIGHT HEART

Jennifer Sodini

ILLUSTRATIONS BY

Natalee Miller

RP **STUDIO**

PHILADELPHIA

RP Studio™
Hachette Book Group
1290 Avenue of the Americas, New York, NY 10104
www.runningpress.com
@Running_Press

Printed in China

First Edition: December 2020

Published by RP Studio, an imprint of Perseus Books, LLC, a subsidiary of Hachette Book
Group, Inc. The RP Studio name and logo is a trademark of the Hachette Book Group.

Design by Josh McDonnell.

ISBN: 978-0-7624-7205-5

LEO

10 9 8 7 6 5 4 3 2 1

Introduction
1

Weeks One through Seven:
The Hermetic Principles
3

Weeks Eight through Ten:
The Alchemical Principles
31

Weeks Eleven through Fifty-Two:
The 42 Ideals of Ma'at
47

This book is dedicated to synchronicity.

The invisible thread of connection, which weaves together the tapestry of our time through space.

While in the process of the weaving the pattern may be difficult to see, however, in retrospect, one can find a vision of divinity in the indivisible grand design of all things.

INTRODUCTION

What can change in a day?
What can change in a week?
What can change in a year?
Everything.

Over the next fifty-two weeks, you'll be going on a journey.

This journey moves through different layers of consciousness, perception, imagination, and will, and your intention throughout will be to evolve into a version of yourself that feels most aligned with your highest vision. This journal will open your heart and mind to an expanded perspective of how consciousness actively creates, shapes, and corresponds with reality.

> In the Emerald Tablets, the Halls of Amenti are described as a space between worlds where time collides and past, present, and future potentials coexist. It is a crystallized codex of consciousness, which is simultaneously a hall of records and a plane of reality. This mysterious space can find its closest correspondence in the notion of the Akashic Records. The Akashic Records, like the Halls of Amenti, are viewed to be a treasury of time, which stores all of the lives, memories, emotions, actions, intentions, and moments of the human and planetary experience (as well as evolution).
>
> *Amenti Oracle: Feather Heart Deck and Guidebook*

Amenti, as a living concept, is the vehicle we will use to move through this journey. Exploring Hermeticism, alchemy, and the embodied ideals of Ma'at, the transformation you are about to embark on will leave you forever changed as you continue to make sense of your own great work.

Everyday Amenti will assist in cultivating a greater understanding of your heart, soul, personality, and purpose. This journal intends to bring you closer to the invisible realms of correspondence that silently guide and direct the life experience. You will transmute your base understanding into a gold foundation, lift heaviness from your spirit as you soar to new horizons, and find your very own feather heart.

THE SEVEN
HERMETIC PRINCIPLES

Weeks One through Seven

When we say a container is "hermetically sealed," it implies that it is airtight. Unbeknownst to many, the word "hermetically" actually has an esoteric origin, dating back to a Greek philosopher known as Hermes Trismegistus, or Hermes Thrice-Great. Hermes has been credited with creating a particular type of glass tube used in alchemy, which is completely airtight. In occult terminology, the metaphor extends further to an implication of airtight, meaning "secret" or "hidden," wisdom.

Hermes, who was also believed to be Thoth (the god of writing and magic) to the Egyptians and Mercury (god of communication) to the Romans, was deemed responsible for a branch of metaphysics called Hermeticism. While this school of thought can be quite complex, there are essential truths that we can pull from it and incorporate into our everyday lives. Hermetic teachings suggest that there is one mind, which corresponds and relates to all things, and can be understood through the observation of correspondence, nature, alchemy, astrology, and theurgy.

The Kybalion, an esoteric book published in 1908 by The Three Initiates, dives deeper into the operations of this secret wisdom by unpacking the governing principles of the universe.

The Seven Hermetic Principles, which we will explore over the next seven weeks, are believed to be those underlying rules, which govern the phenomena of life itself.

As we breathe energy into the mysteries of life through applied practice, we can further our understanding of self in relation to the all.

I The Principle of Mentalism: "The All is Mind; The Universe is Mental."

—*The Kybalion*

The way you begin your day is a reflection of how you live your life. This week let's reflect on the idea that the universe is a reflection of the mind, and take note of how our thoughts speak through our reality.

Over the next seven days, begin each morning by spending five minutes gazing into a mirror and reciting the "I am" mantra of the day. As you speak the words out loud, lean deeply into the intention of the affirmation as you connect to your own image.

Take note of how the affirmation may have inspired a lesson, challenge, or reflection to solidify the meeting of mind to material experience.

Monday:

I am a peaceful presence.

....
....
....

Tuesday:

I am empowered in my power.

....
....
....

Wednesday:

I am an emanation of love's light.

....
....
....

Thursday:

I am a channel through which divine wisdom flows.

....
....
....

Friday:

I am able to achieve with effortless ease.

....
....
....

Saturday:

I am anchored in my awareness.

....
....
....

Sunday:

I am embodied in my highest creative potential.

....
....
....

WEEK TWO

II The Principle of Correspondence: "As above, so below; as below, so above. As the Universe, so the Soul."

—*The Kybalion*

Nature speaks to us, and through us, with the patterns encoded in its grand design. If we stop, look, and listen, there's beauty in all the mysteries that surround us.

This week, take note of the signs you've seen in nature each day.

Reflect on what you see, whether that's a particular flower that caught your eye; a feather you've found on the ground; the weather seeming to echo your emotions; or even how the path a river moves through is the same pattern as the veins beneath your skin, which move your blood.

How is your inner world reflected in the world surrounding you?

III The Principle of Vibration: "Nothing rests; everything moves; everything vibrates."

—*The Kybalion*

Nikola Tesla was once quoted as saying, "If you want to find the secrets of the universe, think in terms of energy, frequency, and vibration." If we distill this idea into an internal application, we may understand that our energy is what we emit into the world from the inside out, our frequency is what we "frequently see," and our vibration is the harmonious movement between mind, body, and spirit.

This week let's test these principles by taking note of how our energy, frequency, and vibration play a role in our day-to-day experiences.

Over the next seven days, have a daily check-in with what you're emitting energetically, frequently seeing (like recurring signs, symbols, or synchronicities), and how attuned your mind, body, and spirit feel.

Place your conscious awareness on how this type of metaphysical movement is made manifest and record any connections you find.

Monday:

Energy: ....

Frequency: ....

Vibration: ....

Field Notes: ....

....

....

Tuesday:

Energy: ....

Frequency: ....

Vibration: ....

Field Notes: ....

....

....

Wednesday:

Energy: ....

Frequency: ....

Vibration: ....

Field Notes: ....

....

....

Thursday:

Energy: ....

Frequency: ....

Vibration: ....

Field Notes: ....

....

....

Friday:

Energy: ....

Frequency: ....

Vibration: ....

Field Notes: ....

....

....

Saturday:

Energy: ....

Frequency: ....

Vibration: ....

Field Notes: ....

....

....

Sunday:

Energy: ....

Frequency: ....

Vibration: ....

Field Notes: ....

....

....

IV The Principle of Polarity: "Everything is Dual; everything has poles; everything has its pair of opposites; like and unlike are the same; opposites are identical in nature, but different in degree; extremes meet; all truths are but half-truths; all paradoxes may be reconciled."

—The Kybalion

2,500 years ago, a mysterious group of mystics known as the Essenes lived on the shores of the Dead Sea in Jerusalem.

They were known to ancient Egyptians as "Therapeutae" (healers), and their spiritual practice emphasized a pure way of life that involved ritual washing, vegetarianism, and the study of the celestial correspondences that exist between earth and the heavens.

In 70 CE, Roman soldiers killed all of the Essenes they could find. The last of the remaining Essene community escaped to Qumran with their sacred scrolls of esoteric wisdom. They lived the remainder of their lives in seclusion and continued to carry out their traditions until fading into obscurity.

Not much was heard of the Essenes until a serendipitous discovery in a town in Upper Egypt known as Nag Hammadi, somewhere between 1946 and 1947.

On this synchronous day, unassuming Bedouin teenage shepherds were tending to their goats, when one of the boys found a collection of large, red, ancient earthenware jars in a nearby cave. In hopes of finding treasure, he opened them and found more than a dozen papyrus codices bound in golden brown leather.

Archaeologists eventually unearthed thousands of such fragments in nearby caves. These codices, which have come to be known as the Nag Hammadi Library, contain close to 900 manuscripts from the secret teachings of the Essenes, including the lost Gospel of Thomas.

In this apocryphal text, the Gospel of Thomas states:

> Jesus said, "Recognize what is in your sight, and that which is hidden from you will become plain to you. For there is nothing hidden which will not become manifest."

This week, in appreciation of the reconciling of paradox, each day we will look into the teachings of the Essenes, in particular the Seven Essene Mirrors.

Each of the daily prompts we offer is intended to assist in deeper insight, as you seek and reflect on the answers hidden within these mirrors.

Monday: THE MIRROR OF THE MOMENT

How is what we are mirroring to those we encounter each day reflected back to us by those we are in relation to (friends, loved ones, co-workers, etc.)?

Today, journal some of the observations that come to mind when considering how your actions are met with reactions, and where a common theme may be emerging.

....

....

....

....

....

....

Tuesday: **THE MIRROR OF JUDGMENT**

What triggers us, and why? How can we actually find healing by looking into the mirror of our judgments?

Today, journal a list of up to ten of your biggest triggers. Then, next to each trigger try and find the lesson, word, or healing modality that may help you resolve this pressure point.

....

....

....

....

....

....

....

....

Wednesday: **THE MIRROR OF LOSS**

"In all of life's uncertainties, one absolute certainty remains: although we live, we shall also die, as we wake, so we shall dream."

In every loss we may find an appreciation for a new life and in darkness, we can learn to reclaim our light—contrast provides sage guidance. Looking to where we have felt lost, or when we have lost something near and dear to us, how can we find new vision in transition?

Today, write a list of some of your greatest "losses," and next to each loss, write something you have learned in the process.

....

....

....

....

....

....

....

Jesus, Lao Tzu, and the Buddha have all been quoted as emphasizing the importance of remaining connected to our "childlike nature."

Through our lives, and experiences, our heart either becomes hardened or lighter, depending on the mindset we approach adversity with.

As a child, we are often free to navigate as avid learners, absorbing the world around us, dreaming big, and imagining even bigger.

Today, in contemplating the mirror of Forgotten Love, take some time to journal about things, feelings, moments, or ways of experience that may have brought you joy in youth, but have disintegrated from adulthood.

Take some time to meditate on what you've written and see how you can integrate and incorporate more of this childlike wisdom into your daily practice moving forward.

....

....

....

....

....

....

....

....

....

....

....

....

....

....

....

....

....

....

In reflecting on the mirror of the Mother and the Father, represented as the sacred energies of the masculine (god, solar, yang, external, forceful) and feminine (goddess, lunar, yin, internal, passive), draw inspiration from strength and balance.

On the left side of this page, reflect on which feminine energies you feel deeply connected to, and then reflect on which energies you would like to work on. At the bottom of your list, write an intention for how you would like to find balance and healing.

On the right side of this page, reflect on which masculine energies you feel deeply connected to, and then reflect on which energies you would like to work on. At the bottom of your list, write an intention on how you would like to find balance and healing.

....

....

....

....

....

....

....

....

....

....

....

....

....

....

....

....

....

Saturday: THE MIRROR OF DARKNESS

In the crevices of consciousness, our trauma, hardship, insecurities, and sadness hide, waiting for us to spelunk our way out of darkness so we can reclaim our light.

Today, look into the caverns of your mind and reach into the darkness for insight. How has the shadow worked its way through your life, and how can you learn to walk with it, instead of having it guide you?

Write out a list of limiting beliefs that have emerged through your mental spelunking. After writing the list of limiting beliefs, illuminate each limitation with empowerment, turning every thought into a diamond by transfiguring excavation into revelation.

....

....

....

....

....

....

Sunday: THE MIRROR OF SELF-PERCEPTION

One of the greatest questions we can ever ask ourselves is "Who Am I?" But who are you, really? Beyond your name, experiences, belongings, desires, relationships . . . who are **you**?

Today, take some time to meditate on your core essence—what makes you *you*—and write down all of the attributes of your soul. Write down all of who you are beyond your labels and reflect on how this divine mirror of self can offer new perspectives of perception.

....

....

....

....

....

WEEK FIVE

V The Principle of Rhythm: "Everything flows, out and in; everything has its tides; all things rise and fall; the pendulum swing manifests in everything; the measure of the swing to the right is the measure of the swing to the left; rhythm compensates."

—The Kybalion

In Disney's *Sword and the Stone*, Merlin teaches the young, future King Arthur this Hermetic ideal through the song, "That's What Makes the World Go 'Round."

This week we will reflect on this principle by examining what makes our world go 'round, and how the rhythm found in opposing forces can connect us to a greater sense of awareness.

Each morning over the next seven days, take some time to drop into a space of presence. Set a timer for five to ten minutes.

Close your eyes and breathe in deeply through your nose. Exhale through your mouth as you work through each daily visualization prompt. After your meditation, reflect on your findings in the space below.

Monday:

How has a moment when I've "fallen" down helped me to rise up into a better version of myself?

....
....
....

What was your reaction?...
What was your response?..
How did you find a resolution?..

Tuesday:

When I've felt as though I've made a wrong choice, how has it actually led me to find the right way?

....

....

....

What was your reaction?..

What was your response?..

How did you find a resolution?..

Wednesday:

When I've felt forgotten, how has this experience helped me remember?

....

....

....

What was your reaction?..

What was your response?..

How did you find a resolution?..

Thursday:

How has a struggle helped me find strength?

....

....

....

What was your reaction?..

What was your response?..

How did you find a resolution?..

How has a poor reaction in the past helped me find better action for the present?

....

....

....

What was your reaction?...

What was your response?...

How did you find a resolution?..

Saturday:

When has a moment when I've been lost actually helped me to find my way?

....

....

....

What was your reaction?...

What was your response?...

How did you find a resolution?..

Sunday:

How can a negative memory that I've been holding in my thoughts be transmuted into a positive memory that I can hold in my heart?

....

....

....

What was your reaction?...

What was your response?...

How did you find a resolution?..

VI The Principle of Cause and Effect: "Every Cause has its Effect; every Effect has its Cause; everything happens according to Law; Chance is but a name for Law not recognized; there are many planes of causation, but nothing escapes the Law."

—The Kybalion

We are coming to learn how thoughts can create experiences, and how our actions inspire reactions.

In connecting deeper to the notion of cause and effect, we seek to grasp how this can cause that.

Over the next week, take conscious note of causation, and reflect on the correspondences you observe.

The "this" list can include thoughts, actions, reactions, or decisions that inspire the "that's," which are the responses that have happened in correlation with the activity.

At the end of each list, reflect on how everything adds up, and what the sum of it all means to you.

Monday:

THIS .... THAT ....

....

REFLECTION: ....

....

Tuesday:

THIS .... THAT ....

....

REFLECTION: ....

....

Wednesday:

THIS .... **THAT** ....
....
REFLECTION: ....
....

Thursday:

THIS .... **THAT** ....
....
REFLECTION: ....
....

Friday:

THIS .... **THAT** ....
....
REFLECTION: ....
....

Saturday:

THIS .... **THAT** ....
....
REFLECTION: ....
....

Sunday:

THIS .... **THAT** ....
....
REFLECTION: ....
....

VII The Principle of Gender: "Gender is in everything; everything has its Masculine and Feminine Principles; Gender manifests on all Planes."

—*The Kybalion*

Note from the author: *The Kybalion was first published in 1908, and the archaic language of this principle has since evolved into a new understanding. The gender spectrum transcends the notion of binary, and there are many gradients of spirit within the human soul. While the Seventh Hermetic Principle of* The Kybalion *is considered The Principle of Gender, our understanding of what this means transcends the idea of gender assignment, but rather extends to the available energies that every human being, regardless of gender identity, has the potential to connect to, and come into relationship with.*

In the Egyptian creation story Atum, the first god, was self-created from the void as both male and female, before spitting the first goddess, Tefnut, and god, Shu, from his mouth.

In Hindu tradition, we find Ardhanarishvara as the embodied illustration of Shakti (the feminine aspect of God) and Shiva (the masculine aspect of God). A living synthesis of the Purusha, spirit/consciousness, and Prakriti, matter/disposition.

During Week Four we touched on the notion of masculine and feminine, and looked at these concepts beyond gender identities, but instead as forces of energy to understand and embody.

By exploring the Hermetic Principle of Gender, we will examine how these energies manifest alchemically over the next week.

Monday:

Monday's planetary correspondence is with the Moon. Feminine in nature, the Moon illuminates in darkness and reminds us that even during our phases we are still whole. Her metallic correspondence is with silver, which aims to help you see beyond the veil, in order to find greater clarity.

Today, connect with the energy of the Moon by reflecting on how you've offered light for friends and/or loved ones during moments of darkness. How has your presence provided various apertures of vision through your own unique lens?

Ground it down with silver as the alchemical offering of deeper insight. How can you be what you've been for others in a way that helps you find the light on your path?

....
....
....
....
....
....
....
....
....
....
....
....
....
....
....

Tuesday: ....

♂

Tuesdays correspond with Mars, the planet associated with the God of War. Mars connects with our desire, survival instincts, aggression, and action. Masculine in nature, Mars teaches us how to fight for the ultimate human experience. His metallic correspondence is iron, which aids in the digestion of reality, processing, experience, and finding spiritual nutrition.

Today, connect with Mars by channeling your iron will. How can activating your inner strength allow you to strategically plan and move towards victory?

What do you truly **want**? How will you **will** it into reality? What **actions** do you need to take?

....
....
....
....
....
....
....
....
....
....
....
....
....
....
....
....

Wednesday: ....

Astrologically speaking, when Mercury goes into retrograde, we often hear warnings about communication mishaps, not signing contracts, and technology backfiring. As the god of communication and ruler of Gemini, Mercury can be channeled to your advantage when he's in his power, allowing the flow of information, communication, and technology to operate at the ultimate level. But, when he's out of alignment, it's advisable to close the door to channeling and find your introspection key.

As the metallic essence, Mercury (also known as quicksilver) is one of the Three Alchemical Principles and is able to transform from liquid to solid states. It's no coincidence that to be called "mercurial" means to have swiftly shifting changes in mood and mindset.

Today, let's connect to the positive aspects of Mercury by examining how you're currently moving through the world.

How are your thoughts informing your communication?

How is your communication informing your sense of connection to self, and those around you?

How is your sense of self informing your levels of confidence and posture?

In which ways can you be more flexible?

In which ways can you be more grounded?

....
....
....
....
....
....

Jupiter, the largest planet in our solar system, represents our innermost nature. Astrologically ruled by Sagittarius, he also calls us to connect to our greatest, most expansive, creative visions, as we usher in a deeper connection to flow states and peak experiences.

Tin is Jupiter's metallic correspondence, and is connected to creativity and sexuality. Jupiter, as an archetype, asks us what we are hoping to birth into the world, and how we are growing towards our next phase spiritually, mentally, and physically.

Today, take time to focus on what gives you pleasure and call in what you'd like more of. Connect to a creative practice that feels best to you in the space below—draw a picture, write a poem, craft a spell, or create a collage of your highest aspiration, and charge it with visions of grandeur.

Friday: ....

Venus, goddess of love, custodian of the heart, has dual rulership over Taurus and Libra. She is the embodied balance of decadence and desire and the archetypal reminder of inner and outer beautification, connection to the heart-space, compassion, affection, and adoration. Venus begs us to make no apologies for self-care and caring deeply for others.

Her metallic correspondence to copper anchors in awareness to the anahata (heart) chakra, and is a tool for balancing and integrating acceptance, while also letting go of attachment to expectation.

Today, focus on your pleasure principles and what makes your heart radiate love. Spend today loving yourself and indulging in activities that make you feel good. No apologies! Treat yourself and enjoy this decadent day.

Reflect on this day in the space below.

....
....
....
....
....
....
....
....
....
....
....
....
....

According to myth, Saturn so feared his loss of power that he ate each of his children just moments after their birth in order to hold on to his place in the throne of time. The metaphor extends to the alchemical correspondence, as Saturn, ruler of the physical form, governs the health of the mortal vessel through which we explore time and space.

Saturn relates to the metallic aspects of lead, which works through the archetypes of fear, death, insecurity, mortality, and pain. It's no wonder this metal is the starting point of journeying to golden awareness. Lead is heavy from both a literal **and** metaphorical perspective!

Today, let's focus on connecting to order from chaos, by facing our fears and letting go of the hold they have on our ability to be in the present moment. Take some time to journal about how time currently works for you, and against you.

Where does chaos feel present? How can you call in more order?

Where do you feel rushed? How can you slow down and be in the now?

How can you connect to a deeper sense of security?

What insecurities are you ready to fully release?

....
....
....
....
....
....
....
....
....

Sunday: ....

The Sun is the alchemical King, crowned in gold. He is the divine spark, the shimmering conscious awareness of creation, and the all-seeing eye of all that is.

He is the unification point of consciousness, spirit, and perception. This precious metal, and precious planet, asks us to imbue the infinite intelligence of the universe into all we touch and create.

In astrology, the Sun is the giver of life, shining a light on your earthly path, as you fulfill the template of your unique heavenly essence.

In honor of the Sun's golden wisdom, today we will begin with a morning meditation.

Take some time to find a comfortable space.

Breathe in through your nose, and out through your mouth, as you say out loud:

I invite the light of the Sun to shine through the top of my crown, and down to the bottom of my feet.

I am open to receive the golden wisdom this invitation offers.

May the light of truth offer a divine coronation of consciousness.

May all obscurations preventing me from my highest vision be washed away with your solar rays.

May I be shown how to illuminate my highest embodied presence.

May I be shown how to be the embodiment of warmth.

May my path be illuminated, as I illuminate the path for others.

Now, close your eyes, and envision sunlight washing through every cell of your body. Envision the warmth you feel on a sunny summer day. Feel this energy running through your spirit and radiating through your aura. Remain in this place until you feel satisfied.

Journal what you've received, experienced, felt, or wish to remember from this practice.

....

....

....

....

....

....

....

....

....

....

....

....

....

....

....

....

....

....

....

....

THE THREE ALCHEMICAL PRINCIPLES

Weeks Eight through Ten

Alchemy is the study of the correspondence of our living universe, and the universe our life creates. This art of transformation and transmutation finds the sacred relationship between the mind and the material. We've already explored how the spiritual, astrological, and material all correspond to archetypes and energies, which can be harnessed, and understood, through the alchemical process.

The Three Alchemical principles, or Tria Prima, which are the foundation of this work, are sulfur (soul), mercury (spirit), and salt (body).

A master alchemist grasps the layers of correspondence between these principles in the natural world, through the synthesis of art, metaphor, and science. The pinnacle of achievement, or magnum opus, is the Philosopher's Stone, a fabled substance believed to turn lead into gold or silver.

Over the next three weeks, we will explore an embodied practice of **internal** alchemy by coming to understand this Trinity within our unique expression of the infinite. And the "Philosopher's Stone" we will cultivate in these exercises will be perspective, which can take any base experience, thought, or idea, and transmute it into valuable vision.

31

SULFUR | SOUL | CONSCIOUSNESS | OIL

SOUL (N): the immaterial essence, animating principle, or actuating cause of an individual life.

Ancient Egyptians believed that the soul could be broken down into nine parts, which come together to create the individual whole. These pieces include the physical body, the name or identity, the personality, the double (or animating spirit), the heart, the shadow, intelligence, form, and a combination of spirits that have previously incarnated.

Later, a classical Theosophical text, *The Secret Doctrine*, suggested that the nine aspects of the soul were actually seven, and this concept of "seven-ing" also mirrored an esoteric Indian tradition.

This week, in conjunction with alchemical sulfur as the prompt of inspiration, we will explore the seven parts of the soul's mirrored aspects. Through different daily visualizations, we will come into a deeper relationship with our invisible, and visible, self through meditation and reflection.

Monday:

EGYPTIAN: Kha, body • **INDIAN:** Rupa, form

MEDITATION: I invite the wisdom encoded within my physical form to radiate through my sacred temple. May I be guided to understand how to best care for my vessel, and love the skin I am in.

REFLECTION: ....

....

....

Tuesday:

EGYPTIAN: Ba, the soul of breath • **INDIAN:** Prana, the breath of life

MEDITATION: I invite my breath to reveal how to nurture my life force. I invite each inhalation to fill my lungs with brilliance. I invite each exhalation to wash away what no longer serves. May the winds of beauty carry my soul into crystalline consciousness.

REFLECTION: ....
....
....

Wednesday:

EGYPTIAN: Khaba, shadow • **INDIAN:** Astral, body

MEDITATION: As light shines over my physical body, so the intangible shadow is revealed. May I find wisdom in the non-physical. May I find a path to ascension by coming to understand the subtle body that follows formed formlessness.

REFLECTION: ....
....
....

Thursday:

EGYPTIAN: Akhu, perception • **INDIAN:** Manas, intelligence

MEDITATION: May I be granted the intelligence necessary to make sense of change. May my keen perception allow logical vision to offer insight. May good judgment be granted on my path, so I am best able to discern with the scientific method and mindful consideration.

REFLECTION: ....
....
....
....

Friday:

EGYPTIAN: Seb, ancestral soul • INDIAN: Kama, animal soul

MEDITATION: May I be guided to understand the visions, lessons, and refractions from my lineage that are reverberating through my path. May the souls that once were shine a light on who I am meant to be.

REFLECTION: ....
....
....

Saturday:

EGYPTIAN: Ptah, first intellectual father • INDIAN: Buddhi, spiritual soul

MEDITATION: I breathe deeply into my solar plexus and invite the spirit of creation to echo through my every cell. May I be a divine architect who builds from the blueprint of my soul. May I be given the discipline, motivation, and confidence to construct and assemble the housing of my true Nature.

REFLECTION: ....
....
....

Sunday:

EGYPTIAN: Atmu, divine/eternal soul • INDIAN: pure spirit

MEDITATION: Without beginning or end, the eternal soul is present—infinite, pure, open. I am a light within the greater light, the light which fills the void, allowing all potential to be expressed and experienced. I welcome my divine nature and I welcome my natural divinity.

REFLECTION: ....
....
....

MERCURY | SPIRIT | MIND | LIQUOR

SPIR·IT (N): the nonphysical part of a person, which is the seat of emotions and character.

Now that we've identified the aspects of your soul, and reflected on their essence through meditation, we will explore the mercurial aspects of spirit—our emotions. In particular, we will see how our moods inform our character or disconnect us from ease.

During the Renaissance period, an alchemist, astrologer, and physician named Paracelsus was a pioneer of the medical revolution. Within his understanding of health and wellness lay the notion that all disease or "dis-ease" stemmed from one of five "entities" (or Ens).

ENS ASTRALE, "ENTITY OF ASTROLOGY": The Ens Astrale relates to the notion of how our surrounding conditions are an externalization of the stars, and how our astrological chart plays an important role in the understanding of our inner and outer worlds.

ENS NATURALE, "ENTITY OF NATURE": The Ens Naturale relates to conditions we may have inherited genetically from our parents, and what has a natural disposition to manifest.

ENS VENENI, "ENTITY OF POISON": The Ens Veneni relates to poisons, toxins, and impurities within our food that cause issues within the digestive system.

ENS SPIRITUALE, "ENTITY OF MIND": The Ens Spirituale relates to spiritual impurities such as emotions, stress, and toxic thinking patterns.

ENS DEI, "ENTITY OF GOD": The Ens Dei is the entity of God, destiny, and karma.

By examining the Ens Spirituale, in particular, as it relates to emotional well-being, we must first identify the seven basic human emotions: happiness, sadness, fear, disgust, anger, surprise, rest (peace).

Each day this week we will focus on how to partner with our thinking patterns to collaborate into wholeness, advance into wellness, and alleviate all dis-ease.

Monday: HAPPINESS

Make a list of what brings happiness to your life.

How often do you get to connect to this emotion, and how does it feel when you are there?

What are some ways you can channel the feeling of happiness by remembering the moments that evoke feelings of ecstasy or serenity?

....

....

....

....

....

....

....

....

....

....

....

....

....

....

....

....

....

Tuesday: SADNESS

In the major arcana of the tarot Temperance (XIV), one of the four cardinal virtues, represents balance, moderation, and flow. In the Rider-Waite iteration of the Temperance card, we see an androgynous angel adorned with the alchemical Sun on their crown, and an orange upright triangle (alchemical fire) inside of a square (the material world) on their chest. With one foot in the water (representing the subconscious), and one on land (representing conscious awareness), the angel holds two cups with which they are diluting wine with water.

Today, let's transmute the times that we have shed tears, by transcending sadness and traveling to Temperance . . . metaphorically turning water into wine.

What have you learned from sadness, and how can you distill it to its essence? Is there a common theme, or a core "ingredient?"

Extract, examine, clarify, and create a new story around what's been bottled up inside.

....
....
....
....
....
....
....
....
....
....
....
....
....
....
....
....

Nothing can paralyze our emotions, and actions, quite like fear. Terror has its tendrils that can assume control of our sense of agency over life, but if we reclaim our power, we empower love and sheer the locks, which blind us.

Today, we will blind our fear, by binding it!

Think of a fear that's taken hold of your life. Contemplate the feeling, and draw it into a design, creature, shape, or abstraction, but don't take up the entire page!

Once you've finished your drawing, create a circle around it. Seal it completely. Look at what you've drawn and say out loud: **"You have no power over me."**

Then shade in the entire drawing within the circle, so there are no visible traces remaining.

Tear this page from your journal, and light it on fire. Take the ashes and empty them into a body of water (ocean, river, lake), or return them to the earth.

Thursday: DISGUST

Believe it or not, disgust can offer a lesson in disguise!

If we contemplate the things, people, places, and objects that we feel repelled by, how can we hold that feeling, even in its discomfort, and find a way to heal it?

First, look at something you feel repulsed by, then think of the core reason.

From a space of nonjudgment, contemplate the actual purpose of each "repulsion's" place in the world (beyond "you"), then offer a "propulsion" by launching it forward with a new perspective. Offer a word of kindness and meditate on a positive quality in what you deem to be negative so you can set it free.

Friday: ANGER

Certain theories posit that anger is actually a secondary emotion—a defense mechanism that creates an icy wall to shield our core vulnerabilities. The "anger iceberg" is a useful visualization, which can show us how anger is the tip of something that runs much deeper.

Today, draw an iceberg or triangular shape, where anger is at the apex. Take some time to reflect on a moment that's made you angry recently. Pause, breathe, look deeper. What were you truly feeling? Write all of the secondary emotions in the space under anger.

Once you've gotten everything out, journal how you feel looking at what's beneath the surface and ponder ways to find deeper catharsis.

Saturday: SURPRISE

Daily ritual can often feel mundane in its monotony.

Wake, shower, eat, work, sleep, repeat.

When we are too rigid in our scheduling, we forget to leave space for spontaneity. Every day offers 86,400 seconds to create systems for your life experience, and how you spend your time is an investment in a future opportunity.

Today, go off the beaten path and be spontaneous!

What surprises did you find by putting stock into an unlikely bet?

....
....
....
....
....
....
....
....
....

Sunday: REST

Breathe into restfulness today! Reflect on what this week's journey through the motions has inspired on your path to deeper awareness and self-knowledge. How do you feel? What would you like to feel more of?

....
....
....
....
....
....
....
....
....

SALT | BODY | STRUCTURED THOUGHT

BOD·Y (V): give material form to something abstract.

If sulfur (the soul) is the perceiver, and mercury (the spirit) is perception, salt (the body) is that which is perceived. Giving form to the formless, salt is the structure of a thought imbued into a body, or form.

In alchemy, metaphor and symbolism allow formations of the formless. Hiding secrets in plain sight, the alchemist uses a symbol as an activator of consciousness, and a means of crafting a universal language that transcends dialect. The body of this work crystallizes consciousness with the image as the key to fluent comprehension.

Over the next week, we will be tapping into the power of the alchemical archetype and the body of an idea.

Monday: THE RAVEN, PUTREFACTION, DESTRUCTION

The raven represents the alchemical process of Nigredo, or putrefaction/decomposition. Metaphorically speaking, this idea extends to the notion that in order for something new to be created, the old form must be destroyed. Destruction is a creative process, creation can at times be destructive.

Today, ponder the raven and consider what you are willing to destroy in order to create something new. How can the process of destruction open space for new levels of creation?

....

....

....

....

....

....

Putrefaction destroys what was and dissolution shows what is, yet this glimpse of light after darkness is superficial in nature. This transformative process is represented by the white swan, a creature we rarely see flying. Instead, they are most often seen floating gracefully on water, skimming the surface, not fully submerged.

It's easy to become enchanted with the allure of the etheric realms, but when your emphasis is only on the exterior, shallow vision lacks the depth that comes from awareness. In the darkness, the ego is putrified, while in the light the nature of self is revealed. In balance we can hold the understanding of this process without attaching judgment to how we come to a conclusion or result.

Today, look past the surface to find the beauty beyond the illusion. Reflect on an instance where an attachment to the superficial may have inspired shallow thinking and/or how a lack of self-awareness can lend itself to eventually knowing a greater awareness of self.

....
....
....
....
....
....
....
....
....
....
....
....
....
....
....
....
....
....
....

Wednesday: PEACOCK, TRANSFORMATION, PERSPECTIVE SHIFT

Light is not the absence of color—light is what allows all colors to be experienced and received through the mind. During the alchemical phase of the peacock's tail, we see the turning point as darkness evolved into the light, which then allowed the unveiling of the rainbow.

Too much time in darkness fills the void with emptiness, while too much time in the light can be blinding.

The peacock can be considered as the symbolic representation of finding appreciation for the colors of change. If we distill the metaphor to its essence, this phase is a call to actualize and remember that anything is possible, and everything has a possibility. But inner work is still necessary to see outer effects.

Today, fix your gaze over the rainbow of transformation. In the process of change, how have you changed into a more conscious creator? What new vision is this evolution allowing in how you view the world around you?

....

....

....

....

Thursday: PELICAN, SELF-SACRIFICE, RECTIFICATION

The symbolism of the pelican in the alchemical process relates to the act of purification and setting things right. Within the coded language, symbolically imbued into the image of this process, we typically will see a mother pelican, who has pierced her breast with her beak in order to feed her young with her own blood as nourishment.

In applying the ideal of rectification through self-sacrifice, reflect on any moments where you've sacrificed yourself in order to help others. How have you grown through the act of sacrifice?

....

....

....

....

Images of the serpent are evocative of the biblical story of the trickster spirit that coerced Eve into eating the forbidden fruit of knowledge in the Garden of Eden. Yet in esoteric tradition, the serpent is sacred, and a symbol of transformation and healing.

The Egyptian cobra goddess Wadjet (meaning "Green One" or "Eye of the Moon") governed time, justice, heaven, and hell, and was revered as the protector of royalty and the land.

Asclepius is the Greek god of medicine, and his rod with a single serpent is used as an image in modern times to symbolize a connection to medical practice.

This image is also linked to Mercury, the god, alchemical symbol, and process.

The serpent is a powerful teacher—guided by its senses, shedding the skin of the past, and moving from coiled presence to fluidly moving awareness.

Today, place your focus on your breath, and how each inhale can uncoil and expand the mind to new awareness, while each exhalation sheds what no longer is serving your highest good.

How has a mindful connection to your breathing awakened any latent energy, or moved any stagnation? Reflect on your findings in the space below.

....
....
....
....
....
....
....
....
....
....
....
....
....
....

Saturday: WHITE UNICORN, SPIRITUAL TRANSITION

Alchemically speaking, the unicorn relates to the intangible, pure, spirit of life, which gives way for resurrection through a transition.

Today, reflect on order from chaos, and how you have found strength through adversity, offering reverence for all of the series of events that allowed you to resurrect after trial and transition.

....
....
....
....
....
....
....

Sunday: OUROBOROS, INFINITY, COMPLETION

The ouroboros is a circular image, which presents a snake, or dragon, eating its own tail. In Egyptian, Greek, Gnostic, and alchemical tradition, it is the symbolic representation of the infinite cycle of life, death, rebirth, the transmigration of souls, and the eternal unity of all things.

This week's journey has given various bodies to alchemical concepts, ideas, and structured thought, with an intention to ground us and connect deeper to the salt of the earth through art and metaphor.

While our answers to these prompts may change in time, as we change through time, which ideas, revelations, or feelings do you beleive you may carry forward as you continue to transform?

....
....
....
....
....
....
....

THE 42 IDEALS OF MA'AT

Weeks Eleven through Fifty-Two

In *The Book of the Dead*, the weighing of the heart is the soul's final judgment, and if the deceased could justifiably answer forty-two specific questions known as the 42 Negative Confessions of Ma'at about how their life had been lived, they could have the choice to pass through to paradise, reincarnate, or if they perfectly answered, become a star—the ultimate destination as the eternal light that fuels the growth of the living universe. If the questions were not answered well and the heart was weighed down from a life filled with regret, negative choices, and actions, then the soul would be damned to be eaten by a chimera-type of demon named Ammit, who devours all the heavyhearted.

The feather by which your heart is measured is the feather of Ma'at, the goddess who is the embodiment of truth, justice, harmony, morality, and the balance of chaos and order.

Amenti Oracle: Feather Heart Deck and Guidebook

Ma'at is an Egyptian goddess, but also a philosophy that seeks a harmonious relationship with life, community, and Earth.

This embodied way of being requires understanding a level of consciousness that revolves around a formula of love (the heart) under the will (conscious attention). If we ponder a vision of the Earth as a school, we may find that time is a teacher, and our curriculum is shaped by studies in direct experience.

So far, we've journeyed through Hermeticism, Alchemy, and various correspondences of energy. And now, over the next 42 weeks, we will explore how to connect to the Ideals of Ma'at.

With the mind of a philosopher, the skill of an alchemist, and the vision of an artist, you will learn how to balance your heart with Ma'at's feather, as you continue to illuminate and expand into celestial awareness.

HONOR VIRTUE

It has been said that the four cardinal virtues are temperance, prudence, courage, and justice—four pillars emerging from a strong spiritual foundation that holds the divine astral architecture of the soul in place.

Looking at virtue as a verb, this week's action step is to make an extra effort to be an exemplary person through random acts of kindness.

Each day this week make an effort to be of service by offering your talent or time to a friend, a stranger, or a loved one—for nothing more than the sake of inspiring more goodness in the world.

Record the actions and reactions your kindness has rippled into the world below.

THE BENEFITS OF GRATITUDE

*A grateful heart is able to navigate the waters of life,
afloat with the lightness of being.*

The more gratitude you express to the world through your love and actions, the more opportunity you offer grace to be echoed back to you.

This week take a daily inventory and give thanks for all the beloved in your life.

Each morning, write out a list of ten things, people, experiences, places, or moments you are grateful for, offering thanks to all that make your heart feel feather-light.

Monday:

Today I am grateful for:...
....

Tuesday:

Today I am grateful for:...
....

Wednesday:

Today I am grateful for:...
....

Thursday:

Today I am grateful for:...
....

Friday:

Today I am grateful for:...
....

Saturday:

Today I am grateful for:...
....

Sunday:

Today I am grateful for:...
....

PEACE

Peace is ease with the dream of creativity and faith in knowing every why will be answered within the hourglass of time.

Peace is ease with the present, which allows us to find the gift in every moment through loving awareness. In allowing consciousness to transcend anxiety, a peaceful mindset opens the opportunity to breathe deeply into the now.

When we are anxious, we are afraid of the future, and depression leaves us lost in the past. Being in the eternal now, we have a chance to remember the precious gift of life and our capacity to create any reality we wish and imagine.

Take ten minutes each morning this week to meditate on the present moment.

Breathing deeply into the heart, and exhaling all that no longer serves you, begin to open space for ease. Allow peace to be your mantra each day, as expanded presence unfolds and echoes through this practice. Record and meditate on what you've learned, below.

Monday:

Mantra: I know peaceful awareness. ....

....

....

....

....

Tuesday:

Mantra: I see with peaceful vision. ....

....

....

....

....

Wednesday:

Mantra: I speak with a peaceful voice. ....

....

....

....

....

Thursday:

Mantra: I offer love, with a peaceful presence to all. ....

....

....

....

....

....

Friday:

Mantra: I inspire peaceful action. ....

....

....

....

....

....

Saturday:

Mantra: I feel at peace today and always. ....

....

....

....

....

....

Sunday:

Mantra: I am complete and at peace. ....

....

....

....

....

....

RESPECTING THE PROPERTY
OF OTHERS

By maintaining a balanced heart and mature mind, we are called to respect the property of others, because there is no 'other' and, as we respect the inner/outer effects of one another, this good karma reflects right back to us.

Honoring the teachers, creators, and magic makers in your life is your current call to action. Pay respect to those who paved the way and opened further pathways of awareness and imaginal insight.

Meditate on the pathways of presence these individuals have emanated into the consciousness of your life, and allow that to shimmer through your spirit during this week's practice.

Create an artistic homage or dedicate the space below to any special teachers, artists, friends, musicians, or philosophers who have helped you on your journey to awareness.

ALL LIFE IS SACRED

Nature's potions and poisons are equally potent, but with the wisdom of an alchemist, even the most poisonous forms of life can be beneficial when the elements are properly manipulated into a medicine.

Superficially it is difficult to distinguish salt from sugar, yet their bitterness and sweetness are understood when tasted.

Bitter medicines can have profound healing capabilities, while an unbalanced intake of the saccharine can cause cavities and cloud the mind.

Well-crafted potions can cause desired effects and well-crafted poisons can affect the desired outcome.

Balance, intention, measurement, careful crafting, and application can turn poisons into potions, but may also turn a potion into poison.

This week let's seek wisdom from bitterness and turn it into sweetness by measuring how the swing in balance can produce a useful application in our lives.

Monday:

What bitterness can you turn into sweetness today?

....
....
....
....

Tuesday:

What bitterness can you turn into sweetness today?

....
....
....
....

Wednesday:

What bitterness can you turn into sweetness today?

....
....
....
....

Thursday:

What bitterness can you turn into sweetness today?

....
....
....
....
....

Friday:

What bitterness can you turn into sweetness today?

....
....
....
....
....

Saturday:

What bitterness can you turn into sweetness today?

....
....
....
....

Sunday:

What bitterness can you turn into sweetness today?

....
....
....
....
....

GENUINE OFFERINGS

While thought and action do echo back into reality and manifest/materialize in some fashion or another, we must be reminded of why we want what we want—and if the reason is to feed the soul or fill a void.

The mind must be an open door to empty space.

What does this riddle mean in relation to genuine offerings?

Well, if we open our minds and hearts to the feeling of what we would like our time to occupy, we can empty an attachment to what that *looks* like, instead exercising actions that help us embody what it *feels* like.

This week feed the soul by practicing thoughts and actions that help foster good karma, and giving offerings without attachment to an end result.

Reflect on how, by trusting inspired action, you have opened your capacity for receiving similar offerings to what you've been giving.

....
....
....
....
....
....
....
....
....
....
....
....
....
....
....
....
....
....
....
....
....

WEEK SEVENTEEN

I LIVE IN TRUTH

The snake sheds its skin when it is no longer necessary, but it is still the same snake transformed. If we remember to shed what is in discord with our truth—as no longer in alignment with our soul's song—we become who we truly are transformed.

This week we will be focusing on how to be usefully, not brutally, honest by acknowledging your authentic feelings, seeking resonance and harmony with your soul's song.

If you find yourself in situations where you may have previously told a half-truth, or half-lie, reconcile the paradox by sharing your honest opinion. Any time you feel inclined to say "no," remember it can also mean "next option." If anxiety is present in your honest expressions, remember the power of your breath, by inhaling strength and exhaling insecurity.

While it may not be easy, if you transmute the uncomfortable feeling of speaking truth into a more aligned connection with confidence, this sincerity will eventually become contagious and magnetize more harmonious experiences and relationships.

How has living in truth been useful on your path this week?

REGARD ALTARS WITH RESPECT

The altar is a sacred space where we pay respect to the elements, artifacts, and teachers who have had a divine impact on our lives within this creative reality.

Life is a ceremony, altar your reality!

If your body is your temple, your home is your own sacred land. Altars help create a method of divine connection by designating an area of our living space to meditation, study, practice, or presence.

Altars can be nondenominational and are not limited to one spiritual belief system.

To create an altar, pick a space in your home where you will be able to connect in peace, free of clutter and heavy traffic. Find or purchase a table, shelf, or desk that fits accordingly.

The altar may be adorned with objects to charge and enhance its intention, including the following:

Sacred books, objects, or icons

Oracle, or tarot, cards

Elements of nature, such as flowers or feathers

Pictures of teachers or loved ones

Candles

White is for purity · Black is for protection · Pink is for love

Red is for passion · Orange is for creative strength

Yellow is for positivity · Green is for abundance

Blue is for forgiveness · Purple is for spiritual connection

Brown is for grounding

Crystals

Incense

This week create your own altar and designate an allotted amount of time to pay your respect and drop into deeper awareness.

Over the next few days record how working with your own altar has helped your sense of connection.

....

....

....

....

....

....

....

....

....

....

....

SPEAK WITH SINCERITY

If we remember the sun as we form our words, the metaphor of light and warmth can shape the context of our communication. The virtue of sincerity in the spoken word can manifest if we lead with solar language.

The winged sun disk is an archetypal symbol of divinity, and power, which has shone through myriad cultures including ancient Egypt, Mesopotamia, Persia, and Greece.

This sun with wings offers an image, which we will conjure in our journey this week, as we give wings to our words and infuse them with warmth.

> The sun speaks to us each day as it rises from the east, its living language uttered in the daily warmth and its light shared without expectation of anything in return.

Each day this week take note of moments where shady words may feel tempting and shine a light by transforming that first thought into something warmer, kinder, or more compassionate.

If you find the shady words come through when thinking of yourself, radiate, transmute, and reclaim your power through your very own solar language.

....

....

....

....

....

....

....

....

....

....

....

....

....

....

....

....

I CONSUME MY FAIR SHARE

. . . we must ask if what we are consuming, or consumed
by, feeds creation or nourishes destruction, and if we are
overindulging by feeding the ego instead of nourishing
the soul.

We have been born into a creative universe, and in the space of creation, consumption follows suit.

Meals are created to be consumed and digested.

Art is crafted to be consumed and appreciated.

Necessity breeds desire and creation fills that void, so it can be utilized by the consumer.

In the cycle of creation and consumption, a fine balance is needed, otherwise we may find ourselves externally surrounded by objects, internally weighed down by our purchases, forever waiting and hoping to feel full from our share.

This week, take note of the balance by placing awareness on how much you create and how much you consume. Reflect on where the scale may be tipping and offer insight on finding equilibrium.

Monday:

What did I create? ....

What did I consume? ....

Where is there space for balance? ....

....

....

....

Tuesday:

What did I create? ....

What did I consume? ....

Where is there space for balance? ....

....

....

....

Wednesday:

What did I create? ....

What did I consume? ....

Where is there space for balance? ....

....

....

....

Thursday:

What did I create? ....

What did I consume? ....

Where is there space for balance? ....

....

....

....

Friday:

What did I create? ....

What did I consume? ....

Where is there space for balance? ....

....

....

....

Saturday:

What did I create? ....

What did I consume? ....

Where is there space for balance? ....

....

....

....

Sunday:

What did I create? ....

What did I consume? ....

Where is there space for balance? ....

....

....

....

....

OFFER WORDS OF GOOD INTENT

Language is a powerful tool with which we can find guidance to navigate infinity, and how we actively, and mindfully, participate in reality is the punctuation to our life's sentence.

It has been said that on average we speak between two thousand and five thousand words each day. When we consider each vibratory signature of our living lexicon and begin to take inventory of the words we find ourselves using most often, there may be a pattern in the way of our words.

Etymology is the exploration of the origin point of words, and the trajectory of how time has influenced and evolved their meaning. The word "philosophy" actually comes from the Greek words *philo* (love), *sophis* (learned system/form of conduct), and *sophia* (knowledge/wisdom). So philosophy holds rooted energy, which corresponds to a love of learned systems of wisdom. Fascinating, right?!

As an exercise this week, take note of your most commonly used terms through time and mindfully explore when/why they come up for you.

At the end of each day, consider your list, and investigate the etymology of your "common words."

Meditate on how each word's origin point may subconsciously inform your attraction to it, then find a replacement word that may be lighter and more aligned with what you're truly seeking to communicate.

PEACEFUL RELATIONSHIP

Human beings are living, breathing metaphors, each a tiny universe, enveloped in the elements.

Stars appear so tiny to humans gazing towards the heavens, yet from the heavens looking down, humanity is microscopic. There's poetry in both perspectives and this week we will explore our own poetic perception of reality.

Urban legend has it that the Nobel Prize-winning author Ernest Hemingway, who many consider the greatest American novelist and writer was once challenged to write an effective story in just six words.

The result, "Baby Shoes For Sale: Never Worn," offers a haunting and cerebral glimpse into a brief flickering of life.

Similarly, a haiku is a Japanese form of micro-poetry, containing just three sentences. The first sentence has five syllables, the second has seven, and the third has five.

For example:

The heart is open,
let us clear our mind and see
how to be here now.

In Zen Buddhism, koans are used to demonstrate a concept or teaching, and to test a student's level of understanding of non-dualism through a puzzle or riddle.

For example:

Teach not talking.

Each day this week write a six-word story, haiku, or koan around the writing prompt offered.

Monday:

Write about your relationship to your heart.

....
....
....

Tuesday:

Write about your relationship to time.

....
....
....

Wednesday:

Write about your favorite feeling.

....
....
....

Thursday:

Write about what your spiritual path means to you.

....
....
....

Friday:

Write about how you perceive yourself.

....
....
....

Saturday:

Write about how you feel others perceive you.

....
....
....

Sunday:

Write about the legacy you'd like to leave behind.

....
....
....

WEEK TWENTY-THREE

I HONOR THE ANIMALS

Bastet, an Egyptian goddess often represented as half feline/ half woman, was worshipped as the safeguard of the pharaoh, the keeper of women's secrets, the goddess of home and childbirth, and the protectress of felines and their caretakers.

The concept of the sacred nature of the animal—not just felines—has rippled through many cultures beyond Egypt, including in the totemic animals of Native American tradition, spirit animals within the shamanic philosophy, as well as spirit familiars in magical practice.

In ancient Greek mythology daemons, not to be confused with demons, were believed to be benevolent nature spirits who guided, protected, and taught humans. In modern myth, author Phillip Pullman's trilogy *His Dark Materials* features daemons as animals, which are an externalized manifestation of a human counterpart's true inner nature.

This week we will look to the animal kingdom to inspire and awaken resonant energies between connected spirits, who may guide, protect, and/or teach us.

Over the next seven days, we will seek to find insight through a visualization exercise that will connect us with our kindred familiar spirit.

Close your eyes and ask to be shown an animal teacher that is most important to your path today. Don't overthink! The first image, idea, or animal that comes to mind, even if it's something unexpected, is the companion that will guide your vision today.

Monday:

What came through? ....

....

....

What message did they have for you? ....

....

....

How did this spirit present itself throughout your day? ....

....

....

Tuesday:

What came through? ....

....

....

What message did they have for you? ....

....

....

How did this spirit present itself throughout your day? ....

....

....

Wednesday:

What came through? ....

....

....

What message did they have for you? ....

....

....

How did this spirit present itself throughout your day? ....

....

....

Thursday:

What came through? ....

....

....

What message did they have for you? ....

....

....

How did this spirit present itself throughout your day? ....

....

....

Friday:

What came through? ....

....

....

What message did they have for you? ....

....

....

How did this spirit present itself throughout your day? ....

....

....

Saturday:

What came through? ....

....

....

What message did they have for you? ....

....

....

How did this spirit present itself throughout your day? ....

....

....

Sunday:

What came through? ....

....

....

What message did they have for you? ....

....

....

How did this spirit present itself throughout your day? ....

....

....

I CAN BE TRUSTED

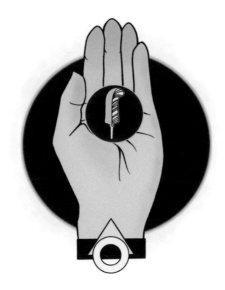

Living always in the light of truth can be challenging in modern times. To attain awareness and protect your values, while still being present in the world, requires a balanced scale.

The Greek myth of Icarus' wings is a timeless tale of the importance of humility, and how hubris can lead to failure. In an attempt to escape from Crete Icarus' father, Daedalus, fashioned wings of feathers and wax. Daedalus warned Icarus not to fly too close to the sun, or too close to the sea, but Icarus did not listen and ascended towards the heavens, only to meet a tragic ending as the wax in his wings melted from the heat of the sun, causing him to tumble into the sea and drown.

In finding cosmic balance in your mind, body, spirit, and life experiences, looking to this myth as a metaphor, you can connect to the importance of not only hearing, but also listening to and trusting, advice intended to increase your awareness.

This week, take note of the moments when you may have been holding onto hubris when given guidance, only to find that the wisdom was actually sound and meant for your highest good.

When has hubris prevented you from trusting guidance?
What has come to light by reevaluating the situation?
How can you fashion new wings of awareness with this wisdom?

....
....
....
....
....
....
....
....
....
....
....
....
....
....
....
....
....
....
....

CARING FOR THE EARTH

A pearl is made when a parasite or a grain of sand finds its way into the shell of an oyster and begins to irritate the insides. From this irritation, the oyster creates an enamel called nacre or mother-of-pearl around the strange visitor, and after some time, the intruder eventually evolves into a pearl.

How can we unearth our irritations, and transform them into iridescent pearls of wisdom?

This week, take an irritation and turn it into inspiration by poetically shifting perspective and using your heart to craft a nacre around the thoughts, things, or people that are getting under your skin.

How can you craft care and ground yourself in what has been unearthed through artful evolution?

Reflect and record your findings!

Monday:

Irritation: ....

Inspiration: ....

Tuesday:

Irritation: ....

Inspiration: ....

Wednesday:

Irritation: ....

Inspiration: ....

Thursday:

Irritation: ....

Inspiration: ....

Friday:

Irritation: ....

Inspiration: ....

Saturday:

Irritation: ....

Inspiration: ....

Sunday:

Irritation: ....

Inspiration: ....

REFLECTION

KEEPING YOUR OWN COUNCIL

The consolation of keeping one's own council comes when the idealized human understands that the mysteries of fate and the manifestations of dreams both spring from the same well: the all-seeing, all-knowing, interconnected mind that is present in every myth and memory.

Every day this week, we will be creating a story using memory as muse. Using the daily prompt as the cup into the waters of the subconscious mind, spring forward into each sentence with the words, "I remember . . ."

Monday: Create a story about your earliest memories.

....
....
....
....
....
....
....

Tuesday: Create a story about the first time you fell in love.

....
....
....
....
....
....
....

Wednesday: Create a story about the first time you experienced heartbreak.

....
....
....
....
....
....
....

Thursday: Create a story about a moment when you've been your own hero.

....
....
....
....
....
....

Friday: Create a story about when you've been a hero to others.

....
....
....
....
....
....

Saturday: Create a story about a time you experienced loss.

....
....
....
....
....
....

Sunday: Create a story about your greatest achievement(s).

....
....
....
....
....
....

SPEAK POSITIVELY OF OTHERS

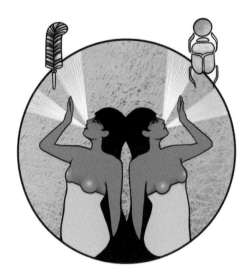

In the book *Initiation, Human and Solar* by Alice A. Bailey, the power of words is perceived to be fivefold, in that each word has varying creative degrees within its essence. Words possess color, tone, form, energy or activity, and the nature of 'the ensouling life, self-conscious, or unconscious, God, man, or deva.'

This week we will take note of the rainbow within our words!

Using your own iteration of this fivefold method, each day record the feelings you're channeling in the light of your words.

Place deep emphasis on positive speech patterns and make a promise to your heart that for the week ahead your words will only be used for the highest good for self and others.

Avoid negative talk, petty conversations, or any form of communication that may be considered detrimental or come back to bite you.

Monday:

WHAT WAS THE RAINBOW OF YOUR WORDS TODAY?

Color: ....

Tone: ....

Form: ....

Energy: ....

Activity: ....

Life Force: ....

Tuesday:

WHAT WAS THE RAINBOW OF YOUR WORDS TODAY?

Color: ....

Tone: ....

Form: ....

Energy: ....

Activity: ....

Life Force: ....

Wednesday:

WHAT WAS THE RAINBOW OF YOUR WORDS TODAY?

Color: ....

Tone: ....

Form: ....

Energy: ....

Activity: ....

Life Force: ....

Thursday:

WHAT WAS THE RAINBOW OF YOUR WORDS TODAY?

Color: ....

Tone: ....

Form: ....

Energy: ....

Activity: ....

Life Force: ....

Friday:

WHAT WAS THE RAINBOW OF YOUR WORDS TODAY?

Color: ....

Tone: ....

Form: ....

Energy: ....

Activity: ....

Life Force: ....

Saturday:

WHAT WAS THE RAINBOW OF YOUR WORDS TODAY?

Color: ....

Tone: ....

Form: ....

Energy: ....

Activity: ....

Life Force: ....

Sunday:

WHAT WAS THE RAINBOW OF YOUR WORDS TODAY?

Color: ....

Tone: ....

Form: ....

Energy: ....

Activity: ....

Life Force: ....

BALANCED EMOTIONS

Remaining in balance with emotions can be a challenge. The head and the heart can at times be in opposition with each other. Like the opposing hemispheres of the brain, logic and feeling don't always agree, yet they must work together in order to function as a whole.

The word "sephirot" means *emanations*, and, according to Kabbalah, there are ten different attributes and emanations through which The Infinite (Ein Sof) reveals itself through creation.

In order to activate a deeper connection to balanced emotion, our intention this week is to connect to the central sephirot, and in turn strengthen the emanations of light within our own energy field.

Monday:

KETHER—CROWN, PURE CONSCIOUSNESS

How may I open to receive pure wisdom, which is enveloped in light and free from ego's myopic perspective?

....

....

....

....

....

....

Tuesday:

DA'AT—KNOWLEDGE, UNIFICATION POINT

How may I find the unification point between my heart and my mind? How can I find knowledge by dropping into this space?

....

....

....

....

....

....

Wednesday:

TIFERET—BEAUTY, GLORY IN BALANCE AND CONNECTION

How may I find equilibrium between logic and intuition, as I meet change with an open heart and stand courageously at the crossroad of all potential?

....

....

....

....

....

....

Thursday:

YESOD—FOUNDATION, CONNECTION

What is currently obscuring my vision, and blocking my sense of connection? How may I shift my thoughts to attract more desirable experiences?

....
....
....
....

Friday:

MALKUTH—KINGDOM, MATERIAL REALM

How can I connect to the most divine aspect of my spirit, so I can call it forth in the material realm? How can I channel my unique expression into inspiration for others?

....
....
....
....

Saturday:

Which emanation did you feel the deepest sense of connection to, and why?

....
....
....
....

Sunday:

How will you continue to connect to a balanced mind, and channel these emanations when you're feeling off-center?

....
....
....
....

TRUSTFUL RELATIONSHIPS

Famed theosophical writer, and one of the first to use the term "new age," Alice A. Bailey also emphasized the notion of 'right human relations' within her occult teachings. As a channel for the Tibetan master Djwhal Khul, she taught that meditation was the vehicle for students to imagine right human relationships by visualizing love and light pouring into all human hearts and minds.

Alice A. Bailey's teachings propose a notion that meditation can be an act of world service, through dreaming of peaceful relationships for all sentient beings. By raising our individual consciousness, we, in turn, raise the consciousness of the lives we touch.

This week, spend some time each day offering a prayer or meditation in service of others, trusting the offering will be received and paid forward with an echo of love and light.

Monday:
I dedicate this practice in service of: ....
....

Tuesday:
I dedicate this practice in service of: ....
....

Wednesday:
I dedicate this practice in service of: ....
....

Thursday:
I dedicate this practice in service of: ....
....

Friday:
I dedicate this practice in service of: ....
....

Saturday:
I dedicate this practice in service of: ....
....

Sunday:
I dedicate this practice in service of: ....
....

HOLDING PURITY IN HIGH ESTEEM

Esteeming purity aligns with knowing the body to be a temple, a sacred space which must be cared for and valued as the house our wisdom and spirit occupy—because as the great William Blake once wrote, "If the doors of perception were cleansed, everything would appear to man as it is, infinite."

Each day this week we will be connecting to, cleansing, and activating a different energy sphere in our body. Breath in the color, and breath out the sound, while focusing on the interconnected energetic intention. Remain in each practice for a maximum of ten minutes. Reflections may be made after the completed session or at the end of your day.

Monday:

THE CROWN OF OSIRIS, HEART, PINEAL, SAHASVARA CHAKRA, LOTUS FLOWER

INHALE: Purple • **EXHALE:** EEE (sounds like "me") • **INTEND:** Awareness

REFLECT: ....
....
....
....

Tuesday:

EYE OF HORUS, BRAIN, PITUITARY, AJNA CHAKRA, SANDALWOOD

INHALE: Indigo • **EXHALE:** AYE (sounds like "say") • **INTEND:** Perception

REFLECT: ....
....
....
....

Wednesday:

THROAT OF THOTH, LUNGS, THYROID, VISHUDDHA CHAKRA, AMBER KASHMIR

INHALE: Blue • **EXHALE:** EYE (sounds like "my") • **INTEND:** Expression

REFLECT: ....
....
....
....

Thursday:

HEART OF ISIS, KIDNEYS, THYMUS, ANAHATA CHAKRA, ATTAR OF ROSES

INHALE: Green • **EXHALE:** AH (sounds like "ma") • **INTEND:** Understanding

REFLECT: ....

....

....

....

Friday:

SOLAR PLEXUS OF RA, GALLBLADDER, PANCREAS, MANIPURA CHAKRA, JASMINE

INHALE: Yellow • **EXHALE:** OH (sounds like "go") • **INTEND:** Will

REFLECT: ....

....

....

....

Saturday:

SPLEEN OF HATHOR, LIVER, OVARIES/TESTES, SVADISTHANA CHAKRA, MUSK

INHALE: Orange • **EXHALE:** OOO (sounds like "you") • **INTEND:** Creation

REFLECT: ....

....

....

....

Sunday:

BASE OF SET, SPLEEN, ADRENALS, MULADHARA CHAKRA, RED AMBER

INHALE: Red • **EXHALE:** UUH (sounds like "cup") • **INTEND:** Anchor

REFLECT: ....

....

....

....

SPREADING JOY

Becoming fluent in the language of spreading joy is an exercise in belief and a study in movement.

In a TED Talk from 2010 Derek Sivers discusses how movements begin by showing a video of one person dancing alone at a concert. Eventually others join this person, and the whole crowd begins dancing, unaware of who began the first movement.

Friedrich Nietzche was once quoted as saying, "those who were seen dancing were thought mad by those who couldn't hear the music."

Laughter yoga, or Hasyayoga, posits that by practicing

prolonged periods of voluntary laughter, you can receive both psychological and physiological benefits—and when done in a group setting, laughter that starts out forced eventually becomes infectious, and the unleashed joy becomes contagious to all who participate.

All this to say, this week our intention is to spread joy through movement, play, laughter, and any activity that tickles the soul and inspires happy thoughts.

Each day this week, commit to joy and reflect on how connecting to light-heartedness has helped your heart feel lighter.

DOING THE BEST YOU CAN

As we actively seek to heal spiritually, restoration comes in unexpected waves that wash over prior perceptions and misconceptions, allowing us the opportunity to evolve from darkness by becoming the best possible people we can be.

"Best" is an ever-evolving concept—there's no end to our evolution—but if we consistently strive to thrive, our lives feel more valuable as we continue to work on self-worth.

Healing, just like the act of achievement, is not a linear or finite process, but with some finesse and focus wholeness may just be on the horizon.

This week pick an area of your life that you'd like to be doing better in, and focus your sight on what that higher vision looks, feels, tastes, sounds, and *is* like.

MY HIGHEST VISION IS:

Every morning reflect on the prompts as pathfinders so you can reach your destination.

Monday:

Have I done my best to achieve my vision? ....

....

How can I do better? ....

....

What do I need to feel my absolute best? ....

....

Tuesday:

Have I done my best to achieve my vision? ....

....

How can I do better? ....

....

What do I need to feel my absolute best? ....

....

Wednesday:

Have I done my best to achieve my vision? ....

....

How can I do better? ....

....

What do I need to feel my absolute best? ....

....

Thursday:

Have I done my best to achieve my vision? ....

....

How can I do better? ....

....

What do I need to feel my absolute best? ....

....

Friday:

Have I done my best to achieve my vision? ....

....

How can I do better? ....

....

What do I need to feel my absolute best? ....

....

Saturday:

Have I done my best to achieve my vision? ....

....

How can I do better? ....

....

What do I need to feel my absolute best? ....

....

Sunday:

Have I done my best to achieve my vision? ....

....

How can I do better? ....

....

What do I need to feel my absolute best? ....

....

COMPASSIONATE COMMUNICATION

Communication and compassion both share layers of meaning and manifestation. Each has the ability to affect through expression and iteration. Looking at their fusion, we may be reminded of the ancient Egyptian goddess Hathor, who was the personification of love, beauty, music, dance, maternal energies, and joy—and is further embodied as the goddess Aphrodite for the Greeks and Venus to the Romans. It was believed that Hathor's heart shone through life, death, transformation, and transfiguration.

A reminder of the virtues of compassion can be found in the suits of the minor arcana of the tarot, which have energetic correspondences to the elements of Hathor's heart.

This week we will focus on compassion in action, by exploring the resonance of the minor arcana's suits, and how you apply empathy in your path and practice.

Monday:

Compassion, like the suit of cups, which may be filled and drank from, is a feeling of relationship to the matter at hand.

REFLECTION: ....
....
....
....
....

Tuesday:

Compassion can be in a thought, like the suit of the sword, which communicates its power through action, and discernment.

REFLECTION: ....
....
....
....
....

Wednesday:

Compassion, like the suit of pentacles, can be a sensation, in the way of a hug or an expression of affection where matter is met with mindfulness.

REFLECTION: ....
....
....
....
....

Thursday:

Compassion, like the suit of wands, is something that can be intuited and expressed through the silent holding of space when it is needed.

REFLECTION: ....
....
....
....
....

Friday:

Which suit of compassion do you resonate with most, and why?

....
....
....
....
....

Saturday:

How can you apply more compassion in your practice and/or path?

....
....
....
....
....

Sunday:

What lesson has reflecting on compassion offered this week?

....
....
....
....
....

LISTEN TO OPPOSING OPINIONS

When we listen to the forces that oppose our comfort
zone instead of fighting them, we can seek wisdom
through opposition by remembering this virtue.

The Five of Pentacles is commonly believed to be one of the least desired cards to pull when doing a tarot reading. The Rider-Waite imagery of the card presents two people who are suffering outside during a snowstorm. Behind them is a church, with a beautiful stained-glass window showcasing five pentacles, which appear in their form to represent the first five sephirot in the Kabbalistic Tree of Life, or perhaps a call to look deeper into the fifth sphere, Gevurah, in particular.

This card traditionally represents hardship, financial woe, and an omen to warn that things may get worse before they're better. But by digging deeper into the symbolism, if we explore the essence of Gevurah as a guiding aspect of the card, the lesson may be finding strength in tough love, overcoming tribulation to triumph, and maintaining faith in the unknown support that may be just around the corner. With Mars and fire ruling this aspect of creation, perhaps we must destroy that which keeps us suffering to create new patterns of presence, finding shelter from the storm.

This week we will step into our "uncomfortable zone" so that we can find wisdom in adversity and see beyond the veil of judgment. Each morning create a list and analyze comfort, discomfort, compromise, and how to find strength in a new perspective.

Monday:

This makes me comfortable: ....

....

This makes me uncomfortable: ....

....

Where is the wisdom in compromise? ....

....

How can this make me stronger? ....

....

Tuesday:

This makes me comfortable: ....

....

This makes me uncomfortable: ....

....

Where is the wisdom in compromise? ....

....

How can this make me stronger? ....

....

Wednesday:

This makes me comfortable: ....

....

This makes me uncomfortable: ....

....

Where is the wisdom in compromise? ....

....

How can this make me stronger? ....

....

Thursday:

This makes me comfortable: ....

....

This makes me uncomfortable: ....

....

Where is the wisdom in compromise? ....

....

How can this make me stronger? ....

....

Friday:

This makes me comfortable: ....

....

This makes me uncomfortable: ....

....

Where is the wisdom in compromise? ....

....

How can this make me stronger? ....

....

Saturday:

This makes me comfortable: ....

....

This makes me uncomfortable: ....

....

Where is the wisdom in compromise? ....

....

How can this make me stronger? ....

....

Sunday:

This makes me comfortable: ....

....

This makes me uncomfortable: ....

....

Where is the wisdom in compromise? ....

....

How can this make me stronger? ....

....

CREATING HARMONY

Harmony can be found or created when we actively seek the relationship between realms of consciousness, matter, and mind by looking for the sustenance within each substance. It is the music of the matrix, if you will.

Our exploration of alchemy has opened our consciousness into understanding the interconnected nature between the various realms of life force.

We've journeyed through the various processes, metaphors, and correspondences, but this week we will seek to "square the circle" and connect to quintessence as the *perceiver*, *perceived*, and *perception*.

Monday ....

The element of fire represents intuition.

How do you currently perceive your relationship to intuition?

How may it better guide what is currently being perceived in your life?

What do you feel you need to stoke this fire of perception?

....
....
....
....
....
....
....
....
....
....
....
....
....
....
....
....
....
....
....
....

Tuesday: ....

The element of air represents thought.

How do you currently perceive your relationship to your thinking patterns?

How may it better guide what is currently being perceived in your life?

How will inspired thinking aid in your sense of perception?

....
....
....
....
....
....
....
....
....
....
....
....
....
....
....
....
....
....
....
....

Wednesday: ....

The element of water relates to feeling.

How do you currently perceive your relationship to your feelings?

How may it better guide what is currently being perceived in your life?

How does feeling inform your sense of perception?

....
....
....
....
....
....
....
....
....
....
....
....
....
....
....
....
....
....

Thursday: ....

The element of earth represents sensation.

How do you currently perceive your relationship to sensation?

How may it better guide what is currently being perceived in your life?

How can sensation inform your current relationship to perception?

....
....
....
....
....
....
....
....
....
....
....
....
....
....
....
....
....
....
....
....
....
....
....

Friday: .... ◯

Quintessence relates to the fifth element, the etheric realm, and is alchemically believed to have great healing powers.

How do you currently perceive your power to heal?

How may your own healing better guide what is currently being perceived in your life?

How can overall healing inform your current relationship to perception?

....
....
....
....
....
....
....
....
....
....
....
....
....
....
....
....
....
....

The Philosopher's Stone is believed to be the greatest work, which contains the elixir of life, enlightenment, bliss, and immortality.

How do you currently perceive your relationship to your life path?

How may your life be perceived as your own Great Work?

How can perception offer an opportunity to find your own sense of enlightened consciousness?

Sunday:

How has what you've learned this week helped to inform the shape of what's to come?

....

....

....

....

....

....

....

....

....

....

....

....

....

....

....

INVOKING LAUGHTER

In honoring this virtue you find resonance with what can best be described as the medicine of the sacred clown, also known as the *heyoka* in Lakota tradition, or the crazy wisdom in Tibetan belief systems.

Aristotle's theory of the humors posits that each of the four elements in alchemy—earth, air, fire, water—governs an aspect of a person's personality and creates its own bodily fluid.

Air (heat and moisture) creates blood, fire (heat and dryness) makes yellow bile, earth (coldness and dryness) makes black bile, and water (coldness and moisture) creates clear phlegm.

Humor is what allows two elements to be joined, creating a byproduct in the process.

So, what does this all have to do with invoking laughter?

Well, comedically speaking, our sense of humor can take one idea and pair it with the opposite to inspire a reaction. There is not one universal comedic formula, but whenever we experience something that is funny to us, laughter is the given byproduct, and at times laughter can be great medicine.

This week, invoke laughter by finding the cosmic jokes in your life's journey. How can you turn tragedy into comedy, and transmute tension into crazy wisdom?

Don't lose faith in the satire! Connect deeply to your own sense of humor over the next few days and record how cultivating laughter has helped you find medicine, even in the drama.

REMAINING OPEN TO LOVE

Embracing *I Am Open to Love in Various Forms* is about understanding, remembering, and embodying love's elements and transitions. It is the deep connection to love as an awareness to become and a detachment from love as a prize to be won or a thing to attain.

This week we will be reflecting on love as a state of consciousness and connect to the awareness of its various forms and processes.

Monday:

Reflect on how love has manifested without thought but as a natural instinct, and what that means to you.

....
....
....
....
....
....

Tuesday:

Reflect on ways you've connected through loving awareness to the family that's not only bound by bloodline, but also by choice.

....
....
....
....
....
....

Wednesday:

How does love inform your perspective on life and death? How does it present itself in your dreams?

....
....
....
....
....
....

Thursday:

How does love work its way through memory and conscious thinking patterns?

....
....
....
....
....

Friday:

How has love been a teacher?

....
....
....
....
....

Saturday:

How has love informed your decisions and/or direction in life?

....
....
....
....
....

Sunday:

How can cultivating more self-love allow you to lift others up to higher ground?

....
....
....
....
....
....

I AM FORGIVING

Keep a feather heart by forgiving and letting go of the density of anger and judgment—a scale is best balanced with light and love.

Ho'ponopono is an ancient Hawaiian practice, believed to have been passed down through oral tradition from wisdom keepers of days gone by. The practice posits that in actively seeking forgiveness for transgressions, the spirit is healed, the gods are pleased, and balance is restored in family, friendships, and community.

In a modern iteration of this ancient medicine, Dr. Ihaleakala Hew Len devised the concept of "Self-I-Dentity thru Ho'ponopono," which has updated the ritual into a simple, yet powerful, exercise.

By stating, "I love you. I'm sorry. Please forgive me. Thank you," to the person from whom you seek forgiveness, you simultaneously forgive and heal yourself.

Each day this week, begin your morning by looking in the mirror and stating the Ho'oponopono mantra out loud to yourself first, then to whomever you would like to offer forgiveness to. If it is helpful, write the words on the mirror with a dry erase marker until the week is complete.

Journal your reflections.

....

....

....

....

....

....

....

....

....

....

....

....

....

....

....

....

....

I AM KIND

Humankind and human kindness are not mutually exclusive, but being a part of humankind does not mean that all of humanity possesses kindness and compassion. We each have a capacity for it, but our ability to express this truly special part of our spirit can at times feel like a great challenge.

Our brains have evolved to contain something called mirror neurons, which, when fired, allow learning through imitation. This type of cognitive mirroring allows us to cultivate a deeper connection to empathy by feeling and reading subtle cues, body language, and emotion.

While mirror neurons open a channel to empathy, so we can feel other's feelings, the current of connection extends further as sympathy helps us understand, and compassion breeds desire to offer relief.

Over the next seven days, reflect on how your actions stoke and kindle kindness. Each day offers an intention for how you'll be embodying empathy, sympathy, and compassion and sparks a fire of inspiration for others to follow.

Monday:

I will exercise empathy in this way:...

....

I will offer sympathy in this way:..

....

I will provide compassion in this way:...

....

Tuesday:

I will exercise empathy in this way:...

....

I will offer sympathy in this way:..

....

I will provide compassion in this way:...

....

Wednesday:

I will exercise empathy in this way:...

....

I will offer sympathy in this way:..

....

I will provide compassion in this way:...

....

Thursday:

I will exercise empathy in this way: ....
....

I will offer sympathy in this way: ....
....

I will provide compassion in this way: ....
....

Friday:

I will exercise empathy in this way: ....
....

I will offer sympathy in this way: ....
....

I will provide compassion in this way: ....
....

Saturday:

I will exercise empathy in this way: ....
....

I will offer sympathy in this way: ....
....

I will provide compassion in this way: ....
....

Sunday:

I will exercise empathy in this way: ....
....

I will offer sympathy in this way: ....
....

I will provide compassion in this way: ....
....

ACTING RESPECTFULLY OF OTHERS

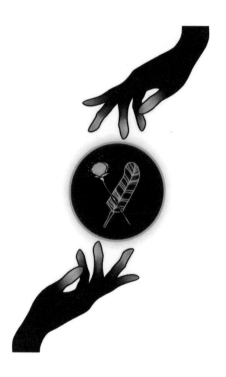

Judge not, love more, and let those who are sleeping dream. Remember to live lucidly within your own conscious imagination, flowing, not fighting.

Ma'at as a living philosophy centers around the embodiment of balance, harmony, truth, justice, order, compassion, and reciprocity. In exploring what it means to walk this path, understanding the moments where we may have lost our footing helps us refocus and become stronger in the process.

In exploring The Mirror of Judgment, we confronted our triggers, and this week we will confront our judgments.

Each day this week, mindfully take note of the moments when you are quick to judge, jump to conclusions, criticize, or have any "I can do it better" thinking.

Reflect on the why, and what can be done to move past judgment and into the heart.

....
....
....
....
....
....
....
....
....
....
....
....
....
....
....
....
....
....
....
....

I AM ACCEPTING

When the sun sets, let us not mourn its temporary slumber while the moon shines in its place. The sun shall rise again when the morning comes. Ebb and flow are the nature of the universe, the cosmic tides of life force washing away the metaphorical sand castles we build with the attention and action we put into the architecture of our lifetime.

An astral temple is an imaginary space of refuge, which can be built in the mind's eye and visited for insight. By practicing creative visualization meditation, and projecting your consciousness into this realm, you can continue to visit, explore, and receive messages beyond this plane of reality.

This week we will explore how to be an architect of awareness by building, discovering, and accepting the messages we may find in the space beyond.

Each day we will place our attention on a different aspect of the room we construct in our imagination. If possible, make this an evening practice as you may receive even more post-meditation, in the dream-space.

Begin each practice with eyes closed and three minutes of rhythmic breathing—inhaling deeply through the nose and exhaling through the mouth. After entering a state of relaxation, we begin to build.

In your mind's eye, imagine a small white cube. Once the cube is in your
vision, expand it, until it becomes a room, no bigger than the size of a
living room.

Now in this completely empty, blank space, imagine the floors to be
checkered black and white. Once you've built the floors, imagine the
walls to the side of you, behind you, and in front of you all having red
velvet curtains that are each drawn closed.

In the middle of this scene, a table appears.

On the table there are two large candles burning on the left and right side,
and in the center there is a book, a fruit, and a flower.

Pick up the book.

What is it?

Put the book down, and now pick up the piece of fruit.

What kind of fruit is it? How does it smell, feel, or taste?

Put the fruit down and pick up the flower.

What does it look like? How does it smell? What will you do with it?

Put the flower down.

Blow the candles out.

Return to awareness and reflect on what you've just experienced—be as detailed
and thorough as possible.

....
....
....
....
....
....
....

In your mind's eye, again, imagine the small white cube. Once the
cube is in your vision, expand it, until it becomes the same room from
yesterday's practice

In the room two chairs appear. One to the left of the room, one to the
right.

The chair to the left is golden, and ornate.

Now the chair is occupied by a male figure. What does he look like? How
does his presence feel? Ask the man what his name is, and if he has a
message for you.

The chair to the right is silver, and ornate.

Now the chair is occupied by a female figure. What does she look like?
How does her presence feel? Ask the woman what her name is, and if she
has a message for you.

Thank them both, and now open your eyes.

Journal your thoughts and reflections, being as detailed as possible.

....
....
....
....
....
....
....
....
....
....
....
....

In your mind's eye, again, imagine the same small white cube. Once the
cube is in your vision, expand it until it becomes the room from our
continuing continued practice.

Now move toward the left wall, looking directly at the curtains. Draw
the curtains open. Behind the curtains is the entrance to a long hallway.
Looking down the hallway, there appear to be various paintings in golden
frames.

Enter the hallway, walk through, and observe the paintings. Stop when
you've found the painting that speaks deepest to your soul.

What does it look like? How does it feel?

Take note of all details.

Walk back down the hallway, out of the entrance and back into the room.
Draw the curtains closed.

Open your eyes.

Journal the different paintings you witnessed, and which painting resonated
most with your soul, being as detailed as possible.

....

....

....

....

....

....

....

....

....

....

....

....

Thursday:

In your mind's eye, again, imagine the same small white cube. Once the
cube is in your vision, expand it until it becomes the room from our
continuing practice.

Now move toward the right wall, looking directly at the curtains. Draw
the curtains open. Behind the curtains is the door to your childhood
bedroom.

Open the door.

Behind the door is the room of your youth. Exactly how it once was.
Unchanged, and frozen in time, but in the center of the room is a wooden
box that resembles a treasure chest. Walk in the room, and open the box.

What's inside? Take note of all the details. Examine, connect, and seek the
relevance of the object.

Put the object back in the box, and close it. Walk out of the room, close
the door and draw the curtain to a close.

Open your eyes.

Reflect on what you found in the box, and how it felt to be in the room.
Remember to be as detailed as possible.

....

....

....

....

....

....

....

....

....

....

....

Friday:

In your mind's eye, again, imagine the same small white cube. Once the
cube is in your vision, expand it until it becomes the room from our
continuing practice.

Now move toward the wall behind you, looking directly at the curtains.
Draw the curtains open. Behind the curtains is a television screen, and its
remote is directly next to it. Turn the television on.

What's playing?

How does it sound, and what does it look like? Does it feel foreign or
familiar?

Observe and reflect until you feel satisfied. Turn the television off, put the
remote back. Close the curtains and open your eyes.

Journal what appeared on the screen, and how it felt to witness it. Remember to
be as detailed as possible.

....

....

....

....

....

....

....

....

....

....

....

....

....

....

....

Saturday:

In your mind's eye, again, imagine the same small white cube. Once the
cube is in your vision, expand it until it becomes the room from our
continuing practice.

Now move toward the wall in front of you, looking directly at the curtains.
Draw the curtains open.

Behind the curtains is a mirror, which is reflecting your true nature, your
core essence. How does it feel? What is it like to gaze directly into your
soul's reflection?

Spend as much time here as you'd like, recording all the details. When
you're satisfied, close the curtains, walk to the center of the room and
open your eyes.

Journal about the lesson in the mirror, and how it felt to witness your essence
on the astral plane.

....
....
....
....
....
....
....
....
....
....
....
....
....
....
....

Now that you've come into a relationship with the astral temple, and
   received tokens of wisdom and explored the cinema of the subconscious,
   let's unpack some of the keys.

In the first vision, the book represents something you need to learn or
   look deeper into, the fruit represents how you perceive opportunity, and
   the flower represents feelings about the future.

The female and male in the chairs are your guides, and can be called upon
   for insight, and protection.

The painting you were drawn to represents a relic from a past life that's
   most connected to your life now.

The treasure chest represents a message from your inner child that can
   help you reconcile something from your past.

The television represents how you feel about the present condition of
   your life.

The mirror represents how you perceive your true self.

With all of this in mind, looking back at your notes, what is the common
   theme, or message that feels most important to work with?

Reflect in the space below.

....
....
....
....
....
....
....
....
....
....

WEEK FORTY-TWO

INNER GUIDANCE

The six integral faculties of mind are believed to be reason, memory, perception, will, imagination, and intuition. The mind's faculties are its metaphorical chess pieces, which assist in strategic navigation over the 'chessboard' of waking life.

This week we are going to work on connecting to, trusting, and activating our "clairs," which are the clear faculties your intuition can move through as you navigate the world around you.

Monday:

CLAIRVOYANCE—"CLEAR SEEING"

Today, invite your consciousness to access clear vision and pay close attention to the signs your sight receives.

RECORD ALL FINDINGS: ....

....

....

....

Tuesday:

CLAIRCOGNIZANCE—"CLEAR KNOWING"

Today, trust your first thoughts, as you are open to receive knowledge and confirmation through clarity.

RECORD ALL FINDINGS: ....

....

....

....

Wednesday:

CLAIRAUDIENCE—"CLEAR HEARING"

Today, invite auricular alchemy to access your awareness. Open your ears to hear the wisdom that may have previously been muted. Tune in, turn on.

RECORD ALL FINDINGS: ....

....

....

....

Thursday:

CLAIRSENTIENCE—"CLEAR FEELING"

Today, invite your feelings to inform the climate of your surroundings. Embodying the empath, seek information from the messages your body is trying to share.

RECORD ALL FINDINGS: ....

....

....

....

Friday:

CLAIRALIENCE—"CLEAR SMELLING"

Today, invite your sense of smell to guide your feelings. Follow your nose and see what perception may be perfumed with guidance.

RECORD ALL FINDINGS: ....

....

....

....

Saturday:

CLAIRGUSTANCE—"CLEAR TASTING"

Today, allow your taste buds to teach you! Savoring this sensation, through conscious connection, what wisdom have you found in mindful relation to taste?

RECORD ALL FINDINGS: ....

....

....

....

Sunday:

Which clair do you feel most connected to, and what did it have to teach you?

....

....

....

CONVERSATIONAL AWARENESS

Mute the mind that wants to make a point to make noise, and take note of where there's room for growth by seeking a conversational melody that balances the exchange of ideas, imagination, emotion, and intellect with a harmony of artistically idealized conversational, conscious awareness.

Sometimes we may find ourselves in situations where we feel unheard, or a partner in conversation may leave you feeling as though they have just been waiting for their turn to talk.

Dialogue is a delicate dance, which at times requires skilled choreography, depending on context, personality, or the overall intention we wish to speak.

This week, take note of when you may have interrupted others, or when you've been interrupted during an exchange of ideas.

How in the process of actively listening can more awareness be placed into the art of conversation?

Record your notes and reflections.

....
....
....
....
....
....
....
....
....
....
....
....
....
....
....
....
....
....
....
....
....

DOING GOOD

Goodness embodied allows for an existence which is history in motion, emotion expressed in the highest form, energy transformed into a testimony of a life lived in alignment with loving-kindness, and a conservation of affection to cause an effect to a world in need.

Loving-kindness is a practice, which has been designed to cultivate feelings of compassion, love, and warm-heartedness. Stemming from the Pali (the sacred language of Theraveda Buddhism) word *Metta*, which means "goodwill" or "loving-kindness," the exercise intends to transform and transfer energy through conscious awareness.

Each day this week, begin with this loving-kindness meditation (no more than ten minutes) to embody goodness and a deeper connection to self-love.

Begin each practice by finding a comfortable position, seated or laying down. Close your eyes and relax into the rhythm of your breath—in through your nose, out through your mouth. Remain in this space for a few minutes without attaching to any thoughts that may pass through. Breathe in peace, breathe out tension. Breathe in relaxation, breathe out the worries of the day. In your mind's eye affirm the following intentions . . .

I am well. · All is well. · I am safe.
All are safe. · I am happy. · May all find their own happiness.
I am peaceful. · All is at peace.

Now, imagine the comfort of a warm bath coursing through your entire body. Visualize emerald green light radiating from your heart and surrounding your aura. Soak in this space until you feel satisfied.

Open your eyes and journal your reflections.

....
....
....
....
....
....
....
....
....
....
....
....
....
....
....
....

GIVING BLESSINGS

Some believe that the act of prayer is when you speak directly to the all that is, while meditation is when the all that is speaks directly to you.

Each day this week we will begin the day with a prayer and end the day with a meditation. Each prayer can be written with your own intention, and each meditation can be as simple as a call for deeper connection, revisiting an exercise from the book, reciting a mantra, or ten to fifteen minutes of silence.

Monday:

MORNING PRAYER: ....

....

EVENING MEDITATION: ....

....

REFLECTIONS: ....

....

....

Tuesday:

MORNING PRAYER: ....

....

EVENING MEDITATION: ....

....

REFLECTIONS: ....

....

....

Wednesday:

MORNING PRAYER: ....

....

EVENING MEDITATION: ....

....

REFLECTIONS: ....

....

....

Thursday:

MORNING PRAYER: ....

....

EVENING MEDITATION: ....

....

REFLECTIONS: ....
....
....

Friday:

MORNING PRAYER: ....
....

EVENING MEDITATION: ....
....

REFLECTIONS: ....
....
....

Saturday:

MORNING PRAYER: ....
....

EVENING MEDITATION: ....
....

REFLECTIONS: ....
....
....

Sunday:

MORNING PRAYER: ....
....

EVENING MEDITATION: ....
....

REFLECTIONS: ....
....
....
....
....

KEEP THE WATERS PURE

The path of self-inquiry and initiation into higher levels of thought and experience asks the candidate to make the unconscious conscious by exploring the abyss of the subconscious mind.

Sobek is the crocodile-headed Egyptian god of the waters, protector of the Nile, and an archetype of our deepest fears.

The Temple of Kom Ombo in Upper Egypt was believed to be a space of reverence for Sobek, which held sacred rituals for neophytes hoping to advance to initiates.

This week we will be diving deeper into the watery abyss of the subconscious, through the creative visualization offered, which we will practice each day. It takes us through an Imaginary Initiation at Kom Ombo, as we come into relationship with what Sobek represents.

Seated in an upright position, close your eyes. Begin to breathe in deeply through your nose, exhaling through your mouth. Practice this cycle of breathing as you relax and melt your cares away.

In your mind's eye visualize yourself inside of a sacred temple. You are now in a chamber looking at a large, circular pool of water surrounded by stone.

Step toward the pool, and dive in.

Swim down, down, down, and deeper until you see two doors.

One door will be shining light, and the other door will appear to be dark.

As you have to make a choice, you feel the presence of crocodiles inching closer and closer. With limited breath, and a choice to risk swimming past the crocodiles, back towards the surface, or select one of two potential portals of escape, what do you choose?

Swim towards your option and take note of what is revealed in the process.

Open your eyes, journal, and reflect.

Monday:

Which door did you enter? What wisdom was revealed?

....

....

Tuesday:

Which door did you enter? What wisdom was revealed?

....

....

Which door did you enter? What wisdom was revealed?

....

....

Which door did you enter? What wisdom was revealed?

....

....

Which door did you enter? What wisdom was revealed?

....

....

Which door did you enter? What wisdom was revealed?

....

....

In what was believed to be the true initiation ritual at Kom Ombo, the twist was that the seemingly safe choice, the light, was actually a dead end. In choosing darkness, you would find air, safety, and new life.

This week did you find yourself moving closer to darkness or light? Was there a common theme? How do you feel this practice has purified the waters in your subconscious mind?

....

....

SPEAKING GOOD INTENTION

The Magician card of the tarot archetypically relates to the planet Mercury, alchemically relates to consciousness and mind, and is expressed through embodiment in the mythology of Hermes Trismegistus, the Thrice-Great.

When we hold our intentions in tension, the ability to manifest our desired result is held in static noise.

If we *will* what we wish, as though it is already here, by speaking in the present tense our will becomes magnetized through the imagination.

This week, when considering a desired result, channel the will of the Magician by creating allusion for the illusions you wish to appear, and speaking as if they already exist.

If becomes *when*, and your "I Am" presence becomes your superpower.

How has shifting wishful thinking to present tense declarations assisted in your journey this week?

Record your thoughts and findings each day.

....

....

....

....

....

....

....

....

....

....

....

....

....

....

....

....

....

....

....

....

PRAISE THE GODDESS AND THE GOD

The word Neter describes the gods and goddesses of Egyptian philosophy. The word itself loosely translates to 'force of nature.'

In Week Four of our journal we discussed the Seven Essene Mirrors, in particular the Mirror of Mother and Father, the divine feminine, and the sacred masculine. During Week Seven, we went on to dive deeper into the essence of these forces from an alchemical perspective, as we explored the astrological and metallic correspondences in various creative practices.

This week, we will dive deeper into embodying these forces of nature by exploring which "Neters of the Now Age" you find deep resonance with, and why.

Over the next week, take some time each day to meditate on which gods, goddesses, artists, creators, teachers, or writers you feel deeply connected to, reflect on which of their qualities speak most to your soul, and then meditate on how you can embody this energy in your presence or practice.

DIVINE FEMININE TEACHERS

WHO	WHAT	HOW?

SACRED MASCULINE TEACHERS

WHO	WHAT	HOW?

WEEK FORTY-NINE
HUMILITY

Are you naked in your authentic truth or are you covered in lies spun from the finest fabric? A humble heart needs nothing more than what it already is.

Some say that the fastest way to win an argument is to admit that you're wrong. Admitting fault is not admitting defeat, but instead can be a tool for growth and a deeper connection to authenticity.

Over the next seven days, take some time each morning to meditate on one moment in your life when ego may have gotten in the way of the heart. Once you have that moment in your mind's eye, write a letter to yourself about how you could have done better, where things may have gone wrong, what you will do better in the future, and what the key lesson/takeaway from this experience may have been.

....

....

....

....

....

....

....

....

....

....

....

....

....

....

....

....

....

....

....

....

....

....

....

....

ACHIEVE WITH INTEGRITY

To the true initiate on the path of studying the mysteries of the universe, wisdom is received through different degrees as the candidate advances past various rituals, tests, and trials, which reveal the worth of the individual found in merit.

The Order of the Eastern Star applies the concept of advancing through different degrees of awareness with various rites of passage. Moving through their symbolic star, a candidate makes a journey to connect to biblical heroines and the seasons their lives represent.

Monday:

ADAH, REPRESENTS THE IDEAL DAUGHTER, THE SEASON OF YOUTH AND SPRINGTIME, AND THE VIRTUES OF FIDELITY, LOYALTY, AND INTELLIGENCE.

How would you like to embody this season and the energies therein?

....

....

....

Tuesday:

MARTHA, EMBODIES THE IDEAL SISTER, THE WINTER SEASON, AND FAITH, TRUST, FORTITUDE, AND THE ENDLESSNESS OF LIFE ETERNAL.

How would you like to embody this season and the energies therein?

....

....

....

Wednesday:

ESTHER, WHOSE NAME LITERALLY TRANSLATES TO "STAR," REPRESENTS THE IDEAL WIFE, AND THE VIRTUES OF LIGHT, POWER, STRENGTH, AND JUSTICE.

How would you like to embody this season and the energies therein?

....

....

....

Thursday:

ELECTA, THE IDEAL MOTHER, EMBODIES THE SEASON OF AUTUMN, AND THE VIRTUES OF HOSPITALITY, HONOR, LOVE, AND DEVOTION.

How would you like to embody this season and the energies therein?

....

....

....

Friday:

RUTH, THE WIDOW, IS THE SUMMER SEASON AND EMBODIES THE TRUE FRIEND WHO ACTS IN HUMBLE SERVICE, HAS AN UNWAVERING DEVOTION TO FAMILY, AND UNDERSTANDS THE POWER OF EVEN THE SMALLEST ACT OF COMPASSION.

How would you like to embody this season and the energies therein?

....

....

....

Saturday:

Claim your name, your energy, your season, your virtues, strengths, and place on your star.

....

....

....

Sunday:

Who did you relate to most this week, and which qualities resonated deepest?

....

....

....

ADVANCING THROUGH YOUR OWN ABILITY

When love takes precedence over fear and wisdom is the primary desire, manifestations fluidly materialize with ease as the light of the sun radiates vision onto the path ahead.

What is something you're still feeling afraid of, and how can you give it love? How can you radiate compassion to the energy that's leaving you constricted, so that you can manifest with effortless ease, and continue to connect to a more expanded presence?

Ideas for your journaling:

I am afraid of you, because of this reason. But, for this exact reason, I am going to give you love, and thank you for allowing me the opportunity to shine a light on my darkness.

What fear has outstayed its welcome? How can you invite it to depart gracefully?

For this reason, I feel as though I am not enough. But, for this reason, I know I am enough.

EMBRACING THE ALL

All is within, but also without, and if you look beyond the surface, you can appreciate this pattern with your every breath. You are the cosmos made conscious, and this moment is but one chapter in a story that never ends.

You've made it through this fifty-two-week journey of self-inquiry and reflection!

Take some time today to journal about how these exercises have transformed your perception and brought you closer to living in alignment with your truth.

Do you feel a deeper connection to a feather-light heart and crystal clear mind?

How has this alchemical transformation changed the way you make sense of the world, galaxy, and universe?

What would you like to continue to record and take note of, so you can anchor in how far you've come and chart a course for how far you'd like to go?

....

....

....

....

....

....

....

....

....

....

....

....

....

....

....

....

....

....

....

....

....

....

....

NOTES

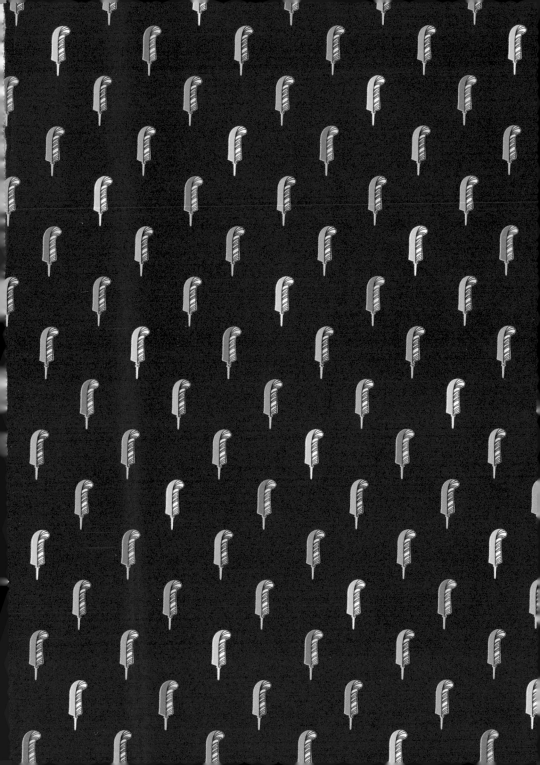